P9-DIY-430

TRANSPORTATION AROUND THE WORLD

By Eleanor O'Connell

Gareth Stevens
PUBLISHING

Please visit our website, www.garethstevens.com. For a free color catalog of all our high-quality books, call toll free 1-800-542-2595 or fax 1-877-542-2596.

Cataloging-in-Publication Data
Names: O'Connell, Eleanor.
Title: Transportation around the world / Eleanor O'Connell.
Description: New York : Gareth Stevens Publishing, 2017. | Series: Adventures in culture | Includes index.
Identifiers: ISBN 9781482455939 (pbk.) | ISBN 9781482455953 (library bound) | ISBN 9781482455946 (6 pack)
Subjects: LCSH: Transportation–Juvenile literature.
Classification: LCC HE151.O54 2017 | DDC 388–dc23

Published in 2017 by
Gareth Stevens Publishing
111 East 14th Street, Suite 349
New York, NY 10003

Designer: Andrea Davison-Bartolotta and Bethany Perl
Editor: Therese Shea

Photo credits: Cover, p. 1 Antonello/Getty Images; pp. 2–24 (background texture) las100/Shutterstock.com; p. 5 Sergey Novikov/Shutterstock.com; p. 7 Anton_Ivanov/ Shutterstock.com; p. 9 RossHelen/Shutterstock.com; p. 11 Kostas Koutsaftikis/ Shutterstock.com; p. 13 Songquan Deng/Shutterstock.com; p. 15 Cristina Stoian/ Shutterstock.com; p. 17 mRGB/Shutterstock.com; p. 19 (Japanese rickshaw) Pabkov/Shutterstock.com; p. 19 (cycle rickshaw) tateyama/Shutterstock.com; p. 21 UKRID/Shutterstock.com.

Printed in China

CPSIA compliance information: Batch #CW17GS: For further information contact Gareth Stevens, New York, New York at 1-800-542-2595.

CONTENTS

Boldface words appear in the glossary.

Ready to Roll?

There's a fair at the park.

Let's go! How would you get there?

Bus? Bike? Car? **Scooter**?

People around the world get from

place to place in some cool ways

you might not have ever heard of!

scooter

bike

5

Camels

Some places need different kinds of **transportation** because of where they are. People ride camels across deserts, such as those in Egypt. Desert sand is hard for cars and other **vehicles** to travel on.

7

Gondolas

Venice is a city in Italy built on many islands. Bridges and **canals** connect parts of the city. Instead of using cars, people use boats to get from place to place! Many visitors to Venice use boats with flat bottoms called gondolas.

Hydrofoils

If you're visiting islands around Greece, you'll want to take a ride on a hydrofoil. These boats use underwater metal plates to lift their **hull** above the water at high speeds. That makes them go even faster!

FLYING DOLPHIN XVII

SEAWAYS

11

Snow Buses

There are special kinds of buses that can move across snow and ice. Some have skis instead of wheels. Some use **tracks**, too. The Terra Bus is a kind of snow bus used in Antarctica and Canada.

Terra Bus

13

Bamboo Trains

The country of Cambodia in Southeast Asia has a special train. The norry (or nori) is made out of **bamboo**. There's only one track for norries. However, a norry can be removed from the track to let another pass.

norry

15

Funicular Railways

Many countries such as Austria have steep mountains a car couldn't drive up. They sometimes have funicular railways. This railway uses a cable to pull a railcar up an **incline**. At the same time, another car on the cable travels down the mountain.

17

Rickshaws

A rickshaw is a cart with one or two wheels. People pull some kinds of rickshaws. They use **pedals** to move cycle rickshaws, like riding a bike. Rickshaws are popular in places such as China and Mexico.

cycle
rickshaw

19

Tuk-Tuks

Some rickshaws have a small engine. They're called auto rickshaws. In Thailand, the auto rickshaw is called a "tuk-tuk" because older kinds had an engine that made a sound like "tuk-tuk-tuk"! Which form of transportation would you like to try?

TAXI

tuk-tuk

21

GLOSSARY

bamboo: a tall grass with hard, hollow stems that are used for building

canal: a long, narrow place filled with water and created by people so that boats can pass through it or to supply fields with water

hull: the deck, sides, and bottom of a boat

incline: a slope

pedal: a flat piece of metal, rubber, or other matter that you push with your foot to make a machine move, work, or stop

scooter: a child's foot-operated vehicle made up of a footboard between two wheels with a steering handle attached to the front wheel

track: a belt on which a vehicle travels. Or, the path on which a vehicle travels.

transportation: a way of traveling from one place to another

vehicle: a machine that is used to carry people or goods from one place to another

FOR MORE INFORMATION

BOOKS

Gaarder-Juntti, Oona. *What in the World Is Green Transportation?* Edina, MN: ABDO Publishing Company, 2011.

Gray, Leon, and Ian Graham. *Transportation.* New York, NY: DK Publishing, 2012.

Walker, Robert. *Transportation Inventions: Moving Our World Forward.* New York, NY: Crabtree Publishing Company, 2014.

WEBSITES

Around the World in 30 Unique Modes of Transport
www.boredpanda.com/transport-modes-around-the-world-fly-to-dubai/
Discover some other kinds of vehicles here.

Vehicle Facts for Kids
www.sciencekids.co.nz/sciencefacts/vehicles.html
Read some cool facts about vehicles.

INDEX